It's Working For Your Good

Embracing Life Lessons While Finding Purpose in Your Pain

Jameelah Henderson, ED.S.

BK
ROYSTON
Publishing

BK Royston Publishing
P. O. Box 4321
Jeffersonville, IN 47131
502-802-5385
http://www.bkroystonpublishing.com
bkroystonpublishing@gmail.com

Cover Design: LS Designs Media Group
Cover Photo: DeNisha McCauley Photography

ISBN-13: 978-1-955063-12-8

King James Version Scriptural Text – Public Domain

New International Version (NIV) - Holy Bible, New International Version®, NIV® Copyright ©1973, 1978, 1984, 2011 by Biblica, Inc.® Used by permission. All rights reserved worldwide.

Printed in the United States of America

Dedication

This book is dedicated to my son Buddy. Because of you, I am forever changed. Thank you for saving my life.

Life Lessons

Introduction

Romans 8:28 And we know that all things work together for good to them that love God, to them who are called according to his purpose. (KJV)

I wrote this book to tell my story…part of it, anyway. The pages of this narrative are filled with details about occurrences that have shaped my identity and magnified God's purpose for my life. I don't share these things for any self-serving reason. Instead, I hope my story serves as a relatable testament to God's enduring love, faithfulness and favor.

Through reading about the peaks and valleys of my life, I hope you're better able to recognize God's voice when He seems untraceable. It is my prayer that you are reminded of the type of God we serve and are compelled to look inwardly as you discover how God can use your experiences to teach you lessons that bring you closer to His will for your life.

So many times, we reach our lowest points and while there, in the thick of our turmoil, can't seem to find God's presence. It's hard for us to comprehend that our traumatizing circumstances are part of a divine plan. Many times, we're unable to fully understand just how God can turn a situation around, but the good thing is we don't have to. That's what makes Him God. We serve a God who knows the purpose He has for our lives and makes all things work toward it.

When your experiences cause you to question your faith, contemplate what testimony lies on the other side of your test. While it's easy to dwell on the life-altering decisions someone made that directly impacted your life, can you challenge yourself to love them anyway? Are you able to show compassion to the person who attacked your character? Can you exhibit empathy for the people who betrayed your trust? Can you resist the temptation to speak harshly to someone who disrespected you? Are you able to maintain your faith in God when it seems like He is silent? Are you able to maintain your peace when every extension of your life feels chaotic? I haven't always answered yes to all of those questions and, even now, I often fall short. Through my trials, however, God has elevated me to a place of enduring contentment and trust in His will.

After reading my story, I hope you are left feeling refreshed, renewed and inspired. I pray that your faith holds tight to the unwavering assurance that no matter what stands before you…it's working for your good.

Lesson 1
Humility

Proverbs 11:2 When pride comes, then comes disgrace, but with humility comes wisdom. (NIV)

I was blessed to grow up in a household that was rooted in faith, love, respect and support. My parents were able to maintain balance, despite sometimes having different approaches to raising my brothers and me. Having friends and family members who were raised in single-parent homes allowed me to, even at a young age, appreciate the value of living with both of my parents. I've never been naive to the sacrifices parents make when raising children. Even as a child, I understood that being a parent was not an easy task, especially when a person does it alone.

Just like many young girls, I too fantasized about my wedding day, dream home and picturesque life as an adult. It was my dream to get married and raise a family in a two-parent household of my own. I promised myself that I would wait until

I was married to have children and would always ensure my children had both parents in their lives. Even as I grew older, I unconsciously judged the single-parent family unit and promised myself that becoming a single mother wouldn't be in my future. I would be married to the father of my children and we would raise our children together as a cohesive unit. I never imagined that becoming a single parent would be part of my destiny. However, that is exactly what happened. As the result of a failed marriage, I became a single mother.

As an outsider, it's easy to view another person's situation and create hypothetical promises to yourself that stem from judgments of someone else's life. The truth is, however, you don't know what you'd do in any given situation until you're actually thrust into it yourself. Have you ever heard about another person's circumstances and said to yourself, "That could never be me"? You know what I mean: that friend who can't muster up the confidence to leave her cheating boyfriend, the coworker who is having an affair, the neighbor in an abusive relationship, the teen parent — and the list goes on. If you think back far enough, I'm sure you can recall a time (or two) when you judged someone else's circumstances.

Prior to my marriage, which has now ended, that judgment crept up when it came to divorce. If someone would have told me that I would one day be a divorced single mother, I would have laughed in their face.

Throughout my early and late 20s, I witnessed many marriages fail and attended a number of lavish weddings to commemorate unions that would last only a few months. I didn't want that to be me. I made a vow with myself that I would not be the girl whose marriage didn't last. Once I said, "I do," it'd be for life.

Who did I think I was? I thought I was in control of my life and future. In no way was I prepared for what would soon transpire and how the very thing that I promised myself would never happen would indeed be the vessel God used to teach me a very tough, but very necessary, lesson in humility.

God's Will

By the age of 31, I had conquered just about everything I had set out to do. I was an award-winning educator and was well on my way to becoming an administrator. I'd even managed to, not just purchase, but build my very first home. I was living my dreams. The way I saw it, God would see fit for me to get married and when He did, my husband and I would live happily ever after. I now realize that marriage simply became a box to check off my internal to-do list. Graduate from college, become a successful educator, build a home, get married. I, pridefully, worked hard to follow the footsteps I thought God laid out for me. Marriage became the obvious and orderly next step.

Before deciding to marry, my partner and I were in a long-distance relationship. We each lived comfortably in our respective birthplaces, just minutes away from family, friends and the comforts of home. As our relationship progressed, so did the reality that one of us would have to uproot our lives. For months, we prepared for the inevitable by weighing the pros and cons of living here or there. Ultimately, we decided I'd be the one to move. And so for the sake of my relationship, future and family, I took a leap of faith, stepped out of my comfort zone and made the sacrifice. I sold my newly-built home, resigned from my job, packed up my belongings and left behind everything and everyone I knew.

After much prayer and many conversations with my loved ones, I was at peace with moving. I felt as though it was God's will and I was confident I'd be rewarded with my happily ever after. The truth is, I did not get married because I was head over heels in love or because I felt it was a God-ordained union. I got married because I thought it was what I was supposed to do at the time. I allowed social trends, internal timelines and superficial expectations to dictate my decisions. I had the mindset that if I did what I thought God wanted me to, then He would do what I wanted Him to do.

Thinking back, I realize I had so much to learn about what it means to live in God's will. Instead of praying for God to direct my path, my prayers consisted of a to-do list of what I wanted Him to do and how I wanted Him to do it. I can imagine God laughing hysterically at me trying to explain to Him the blueprint I'd developed for my life. I could not comprehend it then, but I now understand that God had a plan for my life and He was going to use my fantasy of happily ever after to prepare me for His purpose.

Isolation

It was through the experience of uprooting my life that I began to understand how God was using my situation to enlighten me in new ways. It became clear that God urged me to move because he was preparing me for a destiny that required isolation and separation. What I discovered, and what God already knew, was that being hundreds of miles away from my family and friends was the only way I would begin the journey He was preparing me for. While I was aware that moving to a new place would bring about new beginnings, at the time I did not fully comprehend the magnitude of what God had in store.

Were you ever placed in time-out for being disobedient? Imagine your 6-year-old self-getting in trouble over and over again for breaking the same rule. In order for you to learn the significance of being obedient, you'd have to, time and time again, endure the consequence of your disobedience. While in time out, there are no distractions, no toys and no one to talk to. The goal is that away from all other distractions, children will be compelled to reflect on their actions and consider the choices they've made. They have to make the humble decision to either learn from their choices and not make the same mistake again, or deal with the consequences if they continue the same actions.

For so long, I allowed life to distract me from taking heed to God's will for my life. I devoted the majority of my time and energy to my profession. I distracted myself regularly by finding ways to occupy my time. In retrospect, I wasn't doing this consciously. I didn't wake up in the morning and say "Today, I'm going to go to the mall so I can distract myself." In hindsight, however, that is exactly what was happening.

I wasn't able to fully understand why God said I would be the one to relocate until all of my bags and boxes were moved. I was suddenly isolated, far away from the familiarities of my comfort zone. I knew then…God was sitting me in the corner. He wasn't punishing me. He was preparing and humbling me. God needed my undivided attention, so He got me by myself. While there, He urged me to reflect on the choices I'd made in life and drove me to contemplate whether those decisions were a part of His will. I was being mentally and spiritually matured in ways that would elevate me to new heights and ultimately catapult me toward my purpose.

Due to my independent nature, God was usually not my first point of contact when navigating the muddy waters of life. I preferred to figure things out by calling friends or family members. I'd search the internet a few times, or maybe read a book before I even thought about seeking God for help or direction. He was my last resort. The problem is, I was calling on God *after* exhausting all of *my* resources. The fact is God wanted me to call on Him as my *first and only* resource.

Sometimes we don't realize God is all we need until God is all we have. Initially, being in a foreign place while riding the tide of a failing marriage caused me to feel hopeless. I couldn't understand why God would instruct me to move only to leave me feeling like I was on a planet by myself, miserable and broken. I followed God's direction. How could I possibly be living anything other than my happily ever after? What I didn't know is that everything I thought was going to destroy me was actually being used to strengthen me. And because God orchestrates things in the serendipitous way He does, He used the very situation I had promised myself I would never be in to teach me the ultimate life lesson.

God got my attention in such an undeniable way. I could not confuse anything I was going through as being rooted in anything else but Him. There would be no store runs to make time pass and no going over a friend's house to escape the realities of my home life. God isolated me so that I had no other choice but to lean exclusively on Him.

Can you think of a time when you tried to take matters into your own hands? Did God step in to show you who was actually in charge? If you're anything like me, relinquishing control of your life seems burdensome and nearly impossible. It's frustrating to feel like you're sitting on your hands and allowing life circumstances to just happen to you. You want to fight, think, work and hurry your way out of unforeseen circumstances. This is where humbling yourself and understanding your role comes into play.

As independent and resourceful as we can be, we are still no match to God. It doesn't matter who we know, how intelligent we are or what credentials we have, God has a way of humbly sitting us down and showing us just how magnificent He is.

The truth is, blessings aren't always packaged and wrapped as we expect them to be. God's will for our life is the fulfillment of *HIS* purpose, not ours. We are not the orchestrator of our lives, God is. We are not in control of our destiny, God is. Once we truly start embracing the concept that what He has in store will always be greater than any idea or fantasy we come up with on our own, we can truly begin walking in His purpose and fulfilling our true destiny.

My situation may differ from yours, but think of a time in life when you felt alone or isolated. God just might have been trying to command your undivided attention. You never know how God will get you closer to your destiny, and nine times out of ten, it won't look anything like you'd imagined. As in my case, He might just place you in the situation you said you would never be in just to remind how much you actually need Him.

If you're going through a period of isolation, remain humble and continue to seek God. Ask Him for wisdom, direction and discernment so that you are able to fully hear and stand on His voice and promises. Ask God to open your mind and heart to accept His will over your life, and have peace with every outcome. If you stay focused and remain in His will, God will reveal your destiny and allow you to live in your truth. Even when you can't understand it, it seems impossible, or it seems like you're alone, trust that God is and always will be working for your good.

Lesson 2
Trust

Proverbs 3:5-6 Trust in the LORD with all thine heart; and lean not unto thine own understanding. In all thy ways acknowledge him, and he shall direct thy paths. (KJV)

Trust God

God often uses our difficulties as reminders to trust Him. Often, we get so caught up in our situations that we forget who is sustaining our needs. We put our trust in our family and friends. We put our trust in our careers. We put our trust in what the doctor said or what the government is telling us, and we forget to look to God.

When things are going great in our lives, it's easy to put God on the back burner. We skip a few Sundays of church. We stop reading our Bibles and daily devotionals. I'll admit it: there have been many times when I've become so consumed with controlling my life that I've neglected to pray. I was so busy living life that I got too busy for God. I recall times when I made decisions as though I had life figured out and didn't need to consult God. I made God the head of my life for the big decisions, but didn't consult him when it came to the routine decisions of everyday life. I was trusting in myself and my own understanding instead of leaning on Him. It's when we come to this place in our lives that God will sometimes use our circumstances to get our attention. Not to punish us, but to shift our focus back to Him.

Throughout my divorce, I was only halfway trusting God. I was praying every day, but still looking for ways to control my outcome. I worried myself to the point that I wasn't sleeping, my hair fell out and I was the heaviest I had ever weighed in my life. I was praying, but I wasn't sure God was listening. I knew he would protect me and provide my needs, but I wasn't fully trusting Him with my life. While it is hard to do, we have to let go of our need to control outcomes and resist the temptation to worry ourselves to a frenzy. When we neglect to do so, we lose sight of who we are and *whose* we are.

We are children of the Most-High. As such, we must reach a mental and spiritual place where we allow God to be God. Conditional trust is not what God expects from us. God wants us to wholeheartedly hand over our problems to Him.

Part of the wonder of His greatness is that He doesn't need our help. He's fully capable of dealing with anything thrown His way. The ultimate test for us, as His children, is entrusting Him with our most vulnerable needs, trusting Him when it looks like things aren't going to work in our favor and trusting Him when it seems as if He isn't listening. Many times, it seems like God has left us or no longer hears our prayers. It is when it seems as if God has neglected us, or turned a deaf ear toward our cries, that He is working behind the scenes to orchestrate things on our behalf.

Allow God to fulfill His promises and resist the urge to manipulate what He has predestined. Trusting God doesn't always mean the outcome looks like what we imagined. Trusting God, wholeheartedly, expands our faith and spiritual growth. Just a reminder: There isn't anything we can do that will cause us to miss out on what God has predestined for our lives.

Trust the Process

Find peace in knowing that despite your experiences, God is still able, and in fact wants to do something remarkable in your life. God will impregnate you with possibilities that are beyond anything you can fathom. You simply have to trust His plan during the process.

I know this is easier said than done, but remember that everything that you go through is going to bring you closer to His Will for your life. The business you prayed for, the life you envisioned; it's all within your reach. It may not happen how you thought or when you want, but it will happen. Unfortunately, we live in a world of entitlement and instant gratification. We often confuse delay with denial and get discouraged because things aren't happening as (we) scheduled. Remember, we're not operating on our time, we're on God's time.

We have to stop trying to skip the process to get to the prize. It's like trying to bake a cake without ever putting it in the oven. No matter what ingredients you use, how good of a baker you are or how fancy your kitchen is, if you skip the step of actually putting the cake batter in the oven, you're never going to enjoy the finished product. The process of actually allowing the cake to sit in the oven is the most important step. You have to give the cake time to bake, and even when its baking time is complete, it needs a chance to cool. If you omit one of these key steps, you take the risk of ruining everything you worked so hard for.

Think of going through a tough experience as your cook time. Your knowledge, life experiences and background: that's your cake batter. Just like you can't skip putting the batter in the oven to get the cake, we can't skip going through the work it takes to reach our full potential and fulfill our destiny. The hard work you put in to make it through your experience: that's your bake time. It's going to be uncomfortable. You're going to sweat. There are going to be some days where you feel like giving up. Remember, it's necessary and it'll be worth it. The time you take to allow your cake to cool after it comes out of the oven: that's your healing time. Each step of the baking process is necessary. Each step of your process is critical to who you're becoming. The process is where all the magic happens. Bake your cake!

Trust the Journey

Many times we get so caught up in our destination that we forget to appreciate the beauty of the journey. We ask God to take us places and have the audacity to dictate how He gets us there. Think about your Global Positioning System, or GPS. When you're going to a new location, you put the address in your GPS and trust technology to get you to your final destination. You follow the directions and listen closely to ensure you don't make any wrong turns. You don't wonder how the GPS knew that traffic would be ahead. In fact, you expect it to automatically take that into account when determining the best route. You completely trust the GPS to get you where you need to be. Why is it that we fully trust our GPS, but question God?

Just like our navigation system, God's will is to get us to our final destination…safely and securely. We may have to go down some roads we've never traveled or visit foreign territory for a short time. We may even think we know a better way, so we make a U-turn or take an early exit to get there sooner. But if we trust God to do his job, He will lead us to places that give us freedom to live in His purpose for our lives.

Getting a divorce is a long and strenuous process. The paperwork, disagreements, court visits, costs, not to mention the psychological impact, eventually take their toll. For almost a year, I lived in a constant state of uncertainty, fearing that living away from family and friends would become my permanent destiny. I prayed daily, hoping for the best, but secretly preparing for the worst. Once it was over, I was relieved my divorce was finalized, but extremely overwhelmed with a bevy of emotions. I was overjoyed that I would be back in the close proximity of family and friends, yet embarrassed to be moving home as a single mother. I was excited because I was given the freedom to start over, while at the same time terrified because I had no idea what my future held. My eagerness to move on caused me to ignore the fact that I was not fully healed.

We experience difficult times, persevere through them and become so ready to move on with our lives that we often don't take the time to appreciate the miracle of actually surviving. Healing and restoration are imperative in order to move forward as a whole person. Patience, trust and gratitude are critical components of the healing journey. My circumstances were not ideal, but they were necessary for my growth. It wasn't until I paused to reflect and fully surrendered to His will, that I began to feel true peace. Embracing my healing process allowed me the freedom to fully appreciate where I'd been and where I was going.

God knows what He's doing and where He's taking us. This is the beauty of allowing God to lead. He knows every detour, every obstacle and even the wrong turns we'll take. What's fascinating about God is, though we make wrong turns, He still leads us to our purpose. Don't rush your healing. Embrace your journey and be patient with yourself through the process. Believe that what you are going through is bringing you closer to God's will.

Lesson 3
Perspective

Matthew 5:16 In the same way, let your light shine before others, that they may see your good deeds and glorify your Father in heaven. (NIV)

Don't Miss Your Blessing!

Relocating back to my hometown after my divorce meant I would have to transition back into the school district where I previously worked. I was excited about my return home and the opportunity to reconnect with colleagues and fellow educators. At the same time, there was a seed of bitterness that began to sprout because I equated moving home with taking a step back professionally.

Moving to a new city presented me with the opportunity to attain a leadership role in the school district I was hired in. Going home meant I would have to, yet again, give up something I worked so hard for. First, my marriage…now, my job. I really enjoyed my position and felt the work I did allowed me to thrive in my career. I was grateful to move home, but was still trying to control how things would pan out for me upon my arrival. Initially, I was worried about making enough money to provide for my son and fearful about getting hired at a school, or with an administration. I did not want to work for. The bottom line is, I was afraid of starting over and I wasn't trusting God.

With about 150 schools within its system, the school district in my hometown is enormous. While I could have taken the "I need a job, so I'll take whatever I can get" approach, I, instead, had the nerve to be choosy about where I wanted to work. I only applied for certain positions with certain salaries at certain schools. I tossed around my resume and interviewed here and there to no avail. Once again, I was operating on my own without consulting God. After three unsuccessful interviews, I realized my plan was not going to work. As much as I didn't want to, I was going to have to apply for different positions with lower salaries at schools I didn't *think* I wanted to be.

I have a very supportive network of friends who constantly checked in during my job hunt. In the process of explaining my frustrating job search to one of my friends, I found myself complaining about the positions and schools left for me to apply for. I started to express how much I didn't want to work at these schools because they were in rough neighborhoods and had reputations for attracting challenging student populations. He let me go on and on and then casually asked, "If the population is rough, isn't that a place where those students probably need you the most?" I couldn't do anything but shake my head. He was absolutely right. It was in that moment that my perspective changed. I was reminded why God called me to be an educator in the first place.

When I first began applying for jobs, my choices were rooted in fear, complacency and worry. Initially, my desired salary motivated me to only apply for school leadership positions. I obtained my principal certification years prior and felt I should make the money I thought I deserved.

There was nothing wrong with making the best financial decisions for my son and me. My goal was to ensure my son had a safe, secure and financially stable environment to call home. The issue was that instead of consulting God, I was taking matters into my own hands and gave worry and anxiety full reign over my decisions. My intentions were in the right place. I was, however, operating in survival mode. I was terrified because it wasn't just me I had to be concerned about anymore. I was succumbing to my fears instead of being confident in what God had already called me to do.

I had to start being honest with myself. While I had the credentials and experience to become an administrator, in all actuality, I wasn't mentally ready for everything else that came with such a title. God knew this. I was still dealing with the residual psychological impact of having a baby while in the middle of a divorce. I underestimated the demands of working remotely with a newborn and had not considered the subsequent time commitment and sacrifice of an administration role.

While I didn't know it at the time, God was orchestrating things on my behalf. Not only did I go on to get hired as an instructional coach, but, thanks to my boss at the time, I was also able to continue consulting for the school district for which I was previously employed. I was able to continue doing what I loved without taking a step back in my career and I had multiple streams of income at the same time! Not only did He ensure I was financially secure, but He also worked it out so that I was hired at a school brimming with exemplary instructional leaders.

The leadership team at the school where I was eventually hired is composed of God-fearing women who embody the type of school leader I strive to be. God placed me in a position where I would learn and grow and made sure I was surrounded by people who model and encourage me to walk in my purpose. While I was trying to figure it out, God had already worked it out! I just needed to change my perspective.

It's Bigger Than You

The conversation I had with my friend forced me to remember that my life's purpose is not solely about me, but more about what God can do *through* me. Although these pages are riddled with anecdotes about my own life, this book isn't even about me. God has allowed me to use the lessons I've learned to, hopefully, be a blessing to you in some way.

While at times it's hard to keep at the top of your mind during stressful times, some of your experiences and the lessons you learn from them may have nothing to do with you. Many times, our experiences occur just so someone else can witness what God is capable of.

There are people in your life who watch how you respond to adversity. God is fully aware that your co-worker knows you're dealing with the loss of a loved one and is watching how you cope. God noticed your friend hanging on to your every word when you shared with them the prayer that got you through those sleepless nights. You may have lost your job, suffered from illness or experienced the turmoil of a failing business just so you can be a blessing to someone who can learn from your experiences. Maybe someone will come to know God because of your testimony or gain new confidence in themselves by looking at your life and realizing "if they can make it, so can I."

What if your heartache was so deep because God needed a vessel to show just how well he can mend a broken heart? Maybe you had to lose that job so that others could bear witness to God's sustaining power and provision. Or perhaps you battled and overcame that addiction, so that others would believe that the miracles God performed for you is possible in their own lives.

We are placed on this earth to be a light in the lives of people we encounter. When someone comes into your presence, God wants you to be so consumed by His love that they encounter Him before they see you. Your family, friends, co-workers and neighbors should witness God's love through you. This is your light. It is the positive energy that vibrates from you and is shared through your interactions with other people. Your light is unique to you, and that's what makes it so special. It's what draws others to you.

Use your experiences and the obstacles you've overcome to be a blessing to someone else. Even if it is just one person. Take the opportunity to help others cope with their own battles. Ask God what lessons can be learned from your experiences. Share with others the love, wisdom and blessings you discovered along your journey. How you live your life should be a reflection of the God we serve, not your temporary circumstances.

Lesson 4
Forgiveness

Ephesians 4:32 Be kind to one another, tenderhearted, forgiving one another, as God in Christ forgave you. (ESV)

Forgive the People Who Hurt You

When you've been betrayed by someone, it's very easy to get caught up in pointing blame. Whether it's wanting to let everyone know how wronged you were, or seeking revenge to ensure they feel each and every ounce of pain you felt, if not more, we all in some way want to take redemption into our own hands. Betrayal often leaves a wound that seems impossible to heal. Romans 8:28 reminds us that God has a way of making even the most excruciating pain work for our good and His will.

One of the hardest things we are tasked with in life is forgiveness. We, naturally, hang on to the pain others have inflicted upon us and sometimes have a hard time moving past it. People who are hurting and have not properly dealt with the pain they've experienced need a scapegoat. Unfortunately, the people closest to them often receive the brunt of that pain. As we grow and learn to walk in love and grace, we realize that hurt people hurt people. We can't love God and hate other people. God is love, so when we declare that we love God, that means we also love His children…even His children who may have caused us harm. We have to condition ourselves to extend the same grace to others that God has extended to us.

This is why forgiving others is about you and not the other person. We have no control over other people and how they respond to their experiences. The only person we can control is ourselves. The only actions we can control are our own. We have to acknowledge our own pain and put in the necessary work to heal from past trauma. We must get to a place where what someone does to us doesn't become the poison that taints our personal healing or growth. Holding on to grudges and reliving the hurt someone else caused robs you of your intended future. It forces you to be a prisoner of the past, while the person who hurt you often moves on and lives carefree. This only impedes you from fully enjoying the life God has set out for you. My message to you:

Forgive so you can continue moving on your personal journey of healing and growth.

Let It Go

If you are a parent, you probably know how inquisitive babies are. As a baby, my son loved to roam around on the carpet, explore new toys and independently discover the environment around him. Similar to most babies, he liked to squeeze, slam, and, of course, chew on anything within his reach. When he was about 6 months old, during one of his discovery and sensory sprees, he became frustrated that he couldn't grab a specific toy. This particular toy was new. He tried over and over again to pick it up, but just couldn't put his palm and fingers in the right position in order to do so. As his mother, with one glance, I understood that he was having trouble picking up his new toy because he hadn't yet put down another toy. At 6 months old, my son hadn't yet grasped the concept that in order for him to pick up something new, he was going to have to let go of what he was hanging on to. I'm sure you've figured out where I'm going here.

This scenario is comparable to many things we face in life. You won't fully experience the blessings God has in store for you until whatever it is that you are allowing to hold you back is released. Let it go. While we will surely be confronted with trials, tribulations, pain and hurt, each and every situation we are faced with is nothing more than a glimpse in time. God will use these experiences to teach us life lessons, mature us spiritually and transform us for the better.

Once we've gone through the experience and received the lesson, what's the point of holding on to the pain? Why do we feel the need to continually playback our every hurt and betrayal? It's like watching your favorite movie over and over again and expecting the end to be different. It doesn't make sense and, quite frankly, is a waste of valuable time. Hanging on only hinders you from fully experiencing the joy that can only be discovered when you let go. Close the chapter of anger and resentment and let go of negativity so you can grab hold of the abundance God has in store for your life.

Forgive Yourself

Being betrayed or mistreated by people we love and trust can have, seemingly, an irreparable impact on our spirit and character. My divorce brought out a side of me that I was not proud of. I beat myself up daily by engaging in negative self-talk. I constantly questioned my judgment and regretted my decisions, wondering why I hadn't seen the writings on the wall sooner. I was mean, irritable, bitter and had a constant chip on my shoulder. My anger and pain caused me to have an angry disposition…one where I often found myself lashing out at others. I needed a scapegoat and wanted someone to blame. I wanted people, particularly the person who hurt me, to feel what I was feeling on the inside.

It took some time (many months), but when I changed my perspective and began to look inwardly, I recognized that some of my experiences were a direct result of my lack of boundaries and inability to be honest, with others and myself, about my true feelings. I was looking for someone to blame, but honestly, I needed to do some serious self-reflection. In time, I realized that inflicting pain wouldn't curb, lessen or heal my own. I had to stop nursing my emotional wounds and start using my pain as fuel to begin healing from the inside out.

Forgive yourself for the things you may have said or done to others while going through a storm. We are human. Our emotions run high and can sometimes cause us to make poor decisions. The ability to "turn the other cheek" after being hurt by someone takes patience, self-control and a level of maturity that takes much time and prayer to achieve.

When I compare the girl I was during my teenage and early adulthood years to the woman I am today, there's such a vast difference. As a young girl, I was quick on my feet with witty comebacks, clever remarks and vulgar vocabulary. As I began to mature and become self-aware of the energy I was putting out into the world, I realized that I didn't like the way being mean to others made me feel. I prayed for the Lord to continue to remove the need to always have to confront someone just because they said or did something I didn't like.

This was not easy. I felt like I was constantly being tested, and even backtracked at times — my response to my divorce is the perfect example of such. We have to find the willpower to avoid the trap of becoming entangled in matters that cause us to act or speak out of character. Extend yourself grace when you say things you later regret and, beyond that, ask God for forgiveness. The pursuit of perfection is, more often than not, detrimental to your mental and physical health.

Mistakes are ok.

Did you hear me?

MISTAKES ARE OK.

In fact, mistakes are proof that you are human and that you are trying. The key is learning from those mistakes and using them to fertilize your growth. Remain obedient and trust His promises. Learn to stop giving other people power to disrupt your peace.

Strive for progress, not perfection.

Empathy

Many times, how people treat you is a reflection of what they were (or weren't) taught, how they were raised, the environment they grew up in and the experiences that have shaped their lives.

The realization that the way people treat me is more about them and less about me was a hard, but life changing, concept for me to grasp. I was sad, hurting, angry and didn't know if I had it in me to show compassion. Why should I be expected to show empathy to someone who had not shown empathy to me? As I pondered that question, God answered, "because you're on a personal journey of healing and growth." The Merriam-Webster dictionary defines empathy as "the action of understanding, being aware of, being sensitive to, and vicariously experiencing the feelings, thoughts, and experience of another…." I had to, literally, put my feelings on the back burner and extend grace to the person who caused me so much pain. As part of my growth, I realized that the person who cut me so deeply time and again was fighting their own battles and, unfortunately, I was caught in the middle — a bystander, of their personal storm.

If you've ever been in a situation where you've had to show compassion to someone who hasn't shown it to you, then I'm sure you can relate. If you have not yet been in this situation, keep living. There will come a time in your life where you will be forced to live with the fact that you may never get the apology you feel you deserve. The person who betrayed you may never admit to their faults. Let them deal with the consequences of their actions on their own. The sooner you become empathetic to the people who hurt you, the sooner you can, and will, forgive them.

I will be the first to acknowledge that this is no easy task. Biting your tongue when you want to curse someone out takes control. The moments you feel as though there's no way God would expect you not to defend yourself, are the exact moments He wants you to draw upon your well of empathy and compassion and lean on Him the most.

Pray and ask God to give you the strength you need to face each and every tough situation and person. Just as much as God loves you, He loves the person who hurt you. This might be the last thing you want to hear, but it's true. Being empathetic helps you understand that the person, or people, who hurt you are human too. Just as you are learning to navigate the pain and residual effects of your past experiences, so are they.

Keep the journey you're on and your ultimate goal in life at the forefront of your mind. God wants us to be an example of His love. Yes, even when it's not easy and even when someone else may not be showing that same love to you. Remember, you're on a personal journey of healing and growth. This is bigger than your pain and bigger than the person who caused it. Being empathetic and showing compassion unlocks the door of true peace of mind. Staying focused on who hurt you and how they did so will only keep you stuck in a place that hinders your growth. Stay focused on God and focused on becoming a better you.

Lesson 5
New Beginnings

Jeremiah 29:11 "For I know the plans I have for you," declares the Lord, "plans to prosper you and not to harm you, plans to give you hope and a future." (NIV)

When dealing with stressful situations, I've sometimes made the mistake of believing I could overcome them alone. The fact is, God did not purpose or plan for us to fight our battles alone. If you're anything like me, you've worn yourself out tirelessly swinging, kicking and screaming at your problems, when the entire time God is waiting for you to pass him the boxing gloves. God knows you're exhausted. God knows you're drowning and waiting for Him to throw you a life jacket. Through your troubles, God is refining you. He is building your muscles. He is teaching you how to endure and persevere, even when it seems like the battle is already lost. God is telling you to keep pushing. He will supply your needs and provide you with everything needed to win this battle. He's got you!

Seek Professional Help

If you ever reach that breaking point in life when you feel as though you're at the very end of your rope, call on God and seek professional help. Go to counseling. Find a therapist. I know what you're thinking, people are going to say you're "crazy," or judge you. Right now, I'm giving you every license to throw those thoughts out of the window. Keep in mind why you're doing what you do. You're not going to counseling to appease anyone else. The bottom line is, counseling is the vehicle that will drive you to your healing.

It can be a tough pill to swallow, but life goes on. Clocks keep ticking and the world keeps moving. Your children still need you. Your boss still expects that report by Friday. You still have priorities and obligations that don't stop because you're having a valley moment. What's most challenging about going through a tough time is that it can be overwhelmingly burdensome to maintain and juggle the everyday responsibilities of life. During these times, we often find ourselves running on empty, wounded and unsure about the direction of our lives. These are the areas in life in which counseling professionals thrive.

You're on a mission. Always keep that at the forefront of your mind. When you find a counselor, don't walk, *RUN* to your first session. You have survived traumatic experiences and have endured indescribable pain. I understand that opening up about the messiness, imperfection and deep wounds of your life can be frightening and embarrassing. I know it can trigger anxiety and cause your mind to race miles per minute as you ponder the depths of your discussions. But I promise, once you do the all-important work of finding the right person, it will be one of the most liberating experiences of your life.

You're going to be uncomfortable. You're going to be nervous. You're going to cry. You're going to say to yourself, "What do I say when I get there?" "What's it going to be like?" "What are they going to ask me?" You're going to remember things you thought you'd buried. You're going to be confronted with feelings you weren't aware existed. Your counselor might make you squirm in your seat, but that's their job and it's an indication that you're on the right track. The job of any therapist is to help you acknowledge and realize why you are the way you are and why you respond to things the way you do. They help you get more and best acquainted with yourself. You might not like everything they uncover and you may not enjoy every session, but if they've done their job right, you'll leave each session closer to ultimate healing.

There is a stigma that comes along with going to counseling and therapy, especially in the Black community. Speaking to someone that you don't know about the most personal parts of your life is scary. At my initial session, I was terrified. I, however, reached a pivotal moment in my life where I realized that what I was experiencing was too much for me to try to handle on my own. I knew I'd need to seek professional guidance and that realization was the catalyst that led me to my counselor. I could not articulate the magnitude of my feelings, but at the very least, I knew I was not okay. Seeking out a professional was one of the best decisions of my life.

My counselor helped me learn how to navigate my emotions in a healthy and positive way. She helped me identify what she described as my emotional intelligence, or the ability to become aware of, understand and process my emotions so that I could eventually work through them. Thinking back, had I not made the brave decision to go to counseling when I did, I'm not sure I would have withstood the overloaded weight of my life at the time. I was dealing with a difficult pregnancy while trying to process the fact that I was getting a divorce. On top of that, I was away from my family and support system. Once I gave birth to my son, I had to balance being a new mom, with the psychological and physical effects of postpartum, while also navigating the tough task of working from home during a global pandemic.

WHEW! I was exhausted, defeated and empty. My anxiety was the worst it had ever been my entire life. I was dealing with a lot, but I knew I had to persevere. I had a son whom I had to provide for and who needed his mother to be the best woman she could be. I had no choice but to figure out how I was going to stay spiritually and mentally healthy so that I could be my best self. I sought out a licensed professional counselor who would provide me with coping strategies so that I could live my day-to-day life in the healthiest manner possible.

Of dual importance to me when searching for my perfect therapist was his or her educational and spiritual backgrounds. I needed someone who was in tune with God and would push me to seek Him in the midst of my struggle. My counselor gave me professional resources, but she also prayed with and for me.

The most important relationship you have is the one you have with yourself. Protect it and your mental health at all costs. Just as much as physicians assist us when we're not physically healthy, counselors and therapists help us when we're not mentally healthy. If you're physically sick and over-the-counter medicine no longer works, what do you do? Most people would call a physician. Think of a counselor in the same way. When you're not mentally at your best and you've utilized all of the tools in your personal tool box, seek help from someone who specializes in helping you heal. Keep in mind that you are in the fight of your life and you can't win every battle alone. Seeking help is one of the best things you can do for yourself.

After experiencing a tough time, or even when you're in the middle of one, wouldn't it make sense to seek help from someone who's made healing and helping others their life work? A licensed professional will guide you, help you find your inner peace and hold your hand as you travel to a healthy place of loving, forgiving and understanding yourself and others.

There was no way I would have or could have maintained a sound mind if it weren't for the tools and resources provided to me through routine counseling. I am not telling you that your counselor has to be the same as mine. You have to do what's best for you. Seek guidance from God when searching for someone and He will direct you to who and what you need.

Your Tribe

While being an independent Black woman is admirable, God used the circumstances in my life to humble my independent spirit. There are moments in life when being independent is necessary, and there are moments in life when being independent is unrealistic and downright unhealthy. There's only so much one person can handle alone before the load becomes too heavy. One of the greatest things about God is that He knows what you need and who you need. While the people in your life may not be able to fight your battles for you, God will strategically place individuals in your life to serve as support as you navigate your journey.

Who do you call when you need support? Are the people you interact with pouring into you? Are they telling you the truth? Are they positive and supportive? Do they respect your boundaries? Does their presence create a sense of safety and calmness? Those people, the ones you adamantly proclaimed yes to, are your tribe. It is imperative that you take inventory of the people in your life, especially when experiencing a difficult circumstance.

Pay attention to how you feel when in the company of others. Have you ever spoken to a friend when you're experiencing a tough time and you left the conversation feeling worse? Be mindful of "friends" who seem excited about your difficult time. Sometimes, people find solace in being in the company of others when they don't know how to confront their own situations. Listen carefully. Misery loves company and some people believe a pity party is no party at all if it is experienced alone. It's scary to comprehend, but some people you called a "friend" at the beginning of your journey, might not make it to the end. This can be painful, but it's essential to understand. Unfortunately, there are people in our lives who become dead weight as we grow and evolve. They hold us back by speaking doubt and negativity over our lives. Oftentimes, they are going through their own struggles, and feel better, or in good company, when they witness your struggles.

I truly believe that God speaks to our souls through the Holy Spirit. One of my best friends always says to me, "your gut feeling is your God feeling." God uses the Holy Spirit and our intuition to direct our paths. It is crucial to be hyper-aware of who your advice comes from, particularly when you are going through a stressful time. It's even more critical for your relationship with God to be such that you clearly hear His voice amidst chaos. You need to be able to discern who is in your corner and who is not.

One of the most glorious things about the way God works is that He will use your circumstances to do multiple things in your life. Not only will He use your experiences to elevate you, but He will enlighten you in the process so that you are able to discern who's going to walk into the next chapter of life with you and who needs to remain where they are. You don't have to go out of your way to be rude or mean. It just means you've gained new knowledge about who they are and what they represent in your life. Soon, you will be able to differentiate the roles people have in your life and you will be able to assert boundaries accordingly. As you change, the people around you will change. Don't be afraid to outgrow people.

Self-Care

Do you have hobbies or activities that bring your life joy and peace? Do you have coping skills? How do you make yourself feel better when you're experiencing a stressful situation? Healthy coping strategies are crucial tools to have as you navigate difficult times. When you're going through draining experiences, it's imperative to cope in a healthy and positive way. An idle mind is the devil's playground. Reading a book, binge watching a funny show and writing in a journal are all incredible coping mechanisms. For some, it's taking a social media break and for others it's getting some fresh air on a nice walk. Think about the simple things that bring you joy and weave these activities into your everyday life.

These small, but meaningful, activities will help you persevere. If you are uncertain about what coping skill(s) might work best for you, consult your counselor, therapist or a trusted member of your tribe. They will be able to assist you with identifying the coping skills that are the healthiest and most meaningful for you. Figure out what brings you peace and joy and do those things daily. Your healing depends on it.

Fresh Start

How will your experiences transform your life? Whether good, bad, beautiful, or ugly, everything you experience in life equips you with the tools, knowledge and stamina necessary to walk, survive and excel in your predestined purpose. There's peace in knowing your experience ultimately brings you closer to His will. And in His will, you are victorious.

Embrace your new beginnings. For so long, I couldn't let go of what I had to sacrifice along my journey. I kept repeating to myself, "When this is over, I'm getting my old life back." I found myself reminiscing on memories that were long gone and clinging to a past that no longer existed. I was hanging on to remnants of control that I thought I had over my life. God continuously reminded me that on the other side of this journey was a new woman.

God had to transcend my thinking so He could unveil a new life, a new world and ultimately, a new me. For so long, I missed the point. I was so busy living in the past and hanging on to what I thought I had lost, that I was unable to create space for what was to come. God was trying to take me on the ride of my life and I was so busy

looking back that I almost missed the best part—
a brand new start!

God planted the seed of me becoming an author
more than a decade before I wrote this book. I
knew I was capable, I didn't believe, however,
that I was worthy. So, instead of speaking life into
my dream and watering the seed of limitless
thinking that God had planted within me, I
watered the seeds of fear and self-doubt. Who
would want to read what I have to say? What
would I write about that was different from the
millions of books already published? I allowed
my fear and anxieties to keep me from stepping
out on faith. So, instead of walking in my destiny
and fully embracing the path God set out for me,
I buried the dream of becoming an author so deep
under anxiety and fear that I never imagined it
would come to fruition. I gave up on the idea of
writing and thought God had forgotten about it as
well. I know — it's laughable. How could I
imagine God would ever "forget" anything? If
there's one thing I'm certain of it is this: if God
has placed anything on your heart, He will
provide you with everything necessary for it to
come to pass. I am a living witness to that
sentiment. The fact that you're reading this book
is proof. I began writing to heal. What started
out as a dumping ground for my thoughts in the

notes section of my phone morphed into my first book. I still can't believe it.

Pray your goals and dreams are in alignment with God's will for your life and be willing to put in the work. Goal setting and manifesting is wonderful, but faith without works is dead. Be willing to commit. Don't be so overwhelmed by life's inevitable circumstances that you talk yourself out of what God has promised you. Go for that job. Start your dream business. Go get that degree. Go do what God has called you to do. It's already in you. Hold yourself accountable and stand on God's promises. Instead of focusing on how hurt, battered, and bruised you used to be, consider how resilient, strong and wise you've become.

Embrace the new you and the new journey you are to embark upon. You're now clothed with armor you didn't possess before. You've gained knowledge and wisdom that you didn't have prior to your difficult circumstance. Begin your new journey joyfully and peacefully. You endured the battle of your life and came out victorious! Now that you know better, be compelled to do better. Assert your boundaries. Protect your peace. Live unapologetically in your newly discovered truth. Be confident, bold and unapologetically you.

Exude magic, radiate light and embody love. You are a different person. I dare you to live as such!

Walk in your purpose and be prepared for the path God has set forth for your life. We might not know *what* the future holds, but we certainly know *who* holds our future. What God has in store for you will, without fail, be better than what you left behind. Live a life of joy, happiness and peace in Him. Give yourself the space to learn from your past, discover your truth and prepare for your prosperity. Let your mess become your message, allow your tests to become your testimonies and find purpose in your pain. Prepare for what you pray for. Everything you experience in life is working for your good. Go ahead and let God blow your mind!

Acknowledgements

God: Thank you for a second chance at life. Thank you for reigniting my fire and reminding me why I was put on this Earth. Thank you for living in me, through me, and for me. Everything I am and will be is because of your love, grace, and unwavering favor. Thank you for seeing me, saving me, and keeping me.

Daddy: Thank you for being my constant voice of reason. Thank you for teaching me the value of humility, integrity, and having a personal relationship with God. You taught me how to have discipline, perseverance, and a strong work ethic. Thank you for encouraging me and supporting me, no matter what. I appreciate your guidance and honesty always.

Mama: You are a living example of what it means to put someone else's needs before your own. You've taught me empathy, compassion, and how to love others as God loves us. Thank you for your sacrifice, encouragement, and never ending support. I love you and appreciate you more than words can convey. You are the best mama and nana on Earth!

To my twin, Jimmy: You've been there for every moment of my being-willingly and graciously, without hesitation. My womb-mate and best friend. Thank you for the inside jokes, gut wrenching laughter, and brutal honesty. Thank you for supporting me, believing in me, understanding me, and giving me the space to be vulnerable and free . I don't know what I'd do without you. This book would not exist without you. I thank God for you daily.

To my big brother BJ: There's a level of comfort that can't be explained when you know without a doubt someone is in your corner. Ever since I was a little girl you've been a hero in my eyes. I'm proud of the man you are and the man you're becoming. Thank you for loving me in only the way a big brother can.

A special thank you to my Grandmama: for your prayers that covered me, wisdom that educated me, and faith that continues to inspire me -- thank you! I hope I make you proud.

To my tribe (in no particular order): Jim, Alicia, Lonniea, Ciara, Whitney, Kristeena, Keturah, Dominique, Jewell, Jamaal, Kennetha, Jerron, AJ, Forrest, Dre, Elonka, LaToya, LaTonia, Aisha,Tiffany, Intisar, Daa'iyah, Kendra, Lydia,

& Vaniece: I am forever grateful for you. Whether you were texting to check in, calling to hear my voice, driving hours just to be with me, or simply providing a listening ear…words cannot begin to express my gratitude for you. We each share bonds that feed my soul, speak to my spirit, and challenge me to be better. Thank you for being transparent voices of reason, but never judgmental. Thank you for pouring into me when I didn't have the capacity to pour into myself. Thank you for your loyalty and encouragement. I could not have written this book without your love, support and prayers. I appreciate your consistent friendship in a world that is ever-changing. Thank you.

Jorian: I asked for your help and you didn't hesitate. You are a ray of sunshine and truly a blessing to my life. I am eternally grateful for your keen insight, expertise, and attention to detail. Thank you for your invaluable advice, feedback and suggestions that made my story come together in a way I never imagined. I couldn't have done this without you. I will forever appreciate your ongoing support throughout this entire process and hope to return the favor one day.

Thanks to everyone on the BK Royston Publishing team. Special thank you to Julia for taking the time to ensure I understood the publishing process and helping make my dreams come true. You are appreciated!

A special thank you to Leon, graphic designer and visionary. Your ability to read my mind and create art is a superpower! Thank you for your hard work, patience, and creativity!

DeNisha: What an inspiration you are! Collaborating with you always leaves me feeling empowered and motivated. Thank you for pushing me out of my comfort zone, challenging me, and always making me feel beautiful as ever! You set the bar, honey! Thank you for your light.

Dr. Saudia: Thank you for guiding me through my journey, but giving me the freedom to discover true peace and healing on my own. Thank you for praying with and for me. Because of you, I made it through one of the most challenging experiences I've ever faced. Our sessions together reminded me of God's purpose for my life and challenged me to become a better version of myself. God continuously speaks to me through you, and I am forever grateful.

Lastly, thank *YOU* for taking the time to go on this journey with me. Thank you for giving me the space to be vulnerable, the freedom to be authentic and the autonomy to speak my truth. May you live unapologetically, love authentically, and walk in your purpose daily. Be reminded that every experience, whether good, bad, or ugly is working for your good! Sending you blessings, love, peace, & light.

About The Author

Jameelah Henderson is a full-time educator, educational consultant and author of the inspirational book, *It's Working for Your Good*. She received an Educational Specialist degree and Master's degree from Bellarmine University and a Bachelor's degree from the University of Kentucky. A lifelong learner and self-love advocate, the mother of one uses writing as a form of healing. She is committed to educating, inspiring and empowering others through her work.

When she's not teaching or writing, Jameelah enjoys spending time with her son and creating memories with her loved ones in her home state of Kentucky. Food is her love language; education is her passion; and being a positive light in the world is her mission.

For more information, visit Jameelah online at www.jameelahhenderson.com

www.ingramcontent.com/pod-product-compliance
Lightning Source LLC
Chambersburg PA
CBHW060427050426
42449CB00009B/2175